O. HENRY

The Last Leaf
and Other Stories

Retold by Katherine Mattock

MACMILLAN
CLASSIC

BEGINNER LEVEL

Series Editor: John Milne

The Macmillan Guided Readers provide a choice of enjoyable reading material for learners of English. The series is published at five levels – Starter, Beginner, Elementary, Intermediate and Upper. At **Beginner Level**, the control of content and language has the following main features:

Information Control

The stories are written in a fluent and pleasing style with straightforward plots and a restricted number of main characters. The cultural background is made explicit through both words and illustrations. Information which is vital to the story is clearly presented and repeated where necessary.

Structure Control

Special care is taken with sentence length. Most sentences contain only one clause, though compound sentences are used occasionally with the clauses joined by the conjunctions 'and', 'but' and 'or'. The use of these compound sentences gives the text balance and rhythm. The use of Past Simple and Past Continuous Tenses is permitted since these are the basic tenses used in narration and students must become familiar with these as they continue to extend and develop their reading ability.

Vocabulary Control

At **Beginner Level** there is a controlled vocabulary of approximately 600 basic words, so that students with a basic knowledge of English will be able to read with understanding and enjoyment. Help is also given in the form of vivid illustrations which are closely related to the text.

For further information on the full selection of Readers at all five levels in the series, please refer to the Readers catalogue.

Contents

A Note About the Author

William Sydney Porter was an American writer. He used the name **O. Henry**. He was born on 11th September 1862 in Greensboro, in the state of North Carolina. He did not have much education. He left school at the age of 15.

In 1882, Porter moved to the state of Texas. He worked on a ranch. Then he left the farm and from 1854 to 1886, he was a book-keeper in an office in Austin. He looked after the company's accounts.

William Porter married Athol Estes Roach in 1887. Athol and William had two children, a girl and a boy. Soon, William started writing articles and stories for magazines and newspapers.

Between 1891 and 1894, William worked at the First National Bank in Austin, Texas. In 1895, the police wanted to arrest him. He had taken money from the First National Bank. William ran away from the police and he went to Honduras. He stayed in Central America for a year.

But Athol was very ill and in 1897, William returned to America. Athol died that same year. After that, William was in prison for three years. In the prison, he started writing short stories. Most of them were funny and they had unusual endings.

William Porter came out of prison in 1901. First, he lived in the state of Ohio. Then in 1902, he moved to New York City. William's second wife was Sara Lindsay Coleman. They got married in 1907. William earnt a lot of money, but he spent it all. He drank too much alcohol. William Porter died in a hospital in New York on 4th June 1910. He had only 23 cents in his pocket. He was 48 years old.

Some of William Porter's books are: *Cabbages and Kings* (1904), *The Four Million* (1906), *The Gentle Grafter* (1908) and *Options* (1909).

A Note About These Stories

Times: 1898 to 1910. **Places:** USA – the states in the east and the middle of the country. See the map on page 7.

At the end of the nineteenth century, many people in America had electricity in their homes and businesses. More and more people owned cars. Alexander Graham Bell invented the telephone in 1876. After that, people could speak immediately to each other across long distances. Thomas Edison invented an electric lamp in 1883. Bright lights lit the streets and the houses in the big cities. Fast trains travelled on railroad tracks across America.

O. Henry wrote stories about rich people and about poor people. Some stories are about criminals and detectives. At this time, criminals became cleverer and they travelled further too. They used trains and cars. They escaped from the police easily. Burglars broke into shops and peoples' houses. They stole money and property. Safe-crackers broke into banks. They used special tools and opened the banks' strong metal safes. They stole thousands of dollars.

The police collected a large amount of information about the criminals. These records described the colour of the criminals' hair and eyes, their height, weight and age.

More and more police detectives tried to stop the criminals. Each state had investigators – special policemen who worked for the government. They chased criminals and they investigated crimes. Private investigators worked for clients. The clients paid private investigators to find somebody or something.

Note:

Illinois = ɪləˈnɔɪ

Missouri = mɪzˈʊəri

Arkansas = ˈɑːrkənsɔː

St Louis = seɪnt ˈluːɪs
  (St = Saint)

Greenwich Village =
  ˈgrenɪtʃ ˈvɪlɪdʒ

pneumonia = nuː ˈməʊnɪə

Behrman = ˈbeərmən

Delia = ˈdiːlɪə

Kansas = ˈkænzəs

Peoria = piːˈɔːriːə

Houston = ˈhjuːstən

New Orleans =
  nuː ˈɔːrliːənz

Chicago = ʃɪˈkɑːgəʊ

A Map of the Places in These Stories

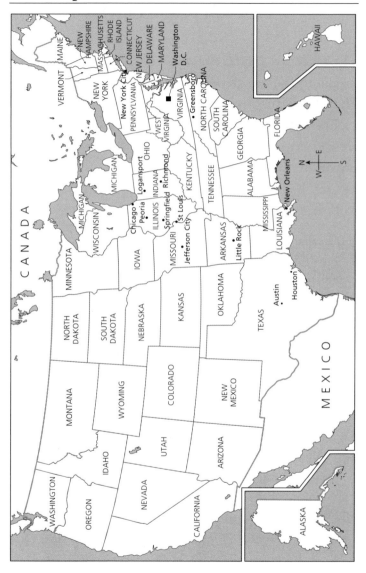

1

A GOOD BURGLAR

The place was North America. The year was 1900.

Jimmy Valentine was in prison. He was Prisoner Number 9762. Jimmy had been in prison for nine months. He wanted to get out of prison and his friends were trying to help him. His friends were talking to important people about him.

One day, Jimmy was making shoes in the prison workshop. A guard came into the room.

'The warden wants to talk to you, 9762,' the guard said. He took Jimmy to the warden's office.

'Valentine, you're a lucky man!' said the warden. 'You have powerful friends. The government has given you a pardon. Tomorrow, you'll be free. Listen to me, Valentine. You are not a bad young man. Don't come back to prison! You can change your life. You must live honestly now. You mustn't steal any more money. Stop burgling! Stop safe-cracking!'

'I'm not a safe-cracker, sir!' Jimmy said. 'I've never cracked a safe in my life!'

The warden laughed. 'Who cracked that safe in Springfield?' he asked. 'Didn't you do that job?'

'Springfield?' Jimmy replied. 'I've never been there in my life!'

'Take him away,' the warden said to the guard. 'Bring him here at seven o'clock tomorrow morning.'

———

Early the next morning, Jimmy was standing in the warden's office again. A prison clerk gave him a railroad ticket and five dollars. The warden shook Jimmy's hand. Then Prisoner Number 9762 became Mr James Valentine. He walked out of the prison, into the sunshine.

Outside the prison, the birds were singing. But Jimmy did not listen to them. He went to a restaurant and he had a good meal – a chicken and a bottle of wine. Then he got on a train.

Three hours later, Jimmy got off the train at a little town in Illinois. He went into a small bar and shook hands with the owner.

'Mike Dolan!' said Jimmy. 'How are you?'

'I'm sorry, Jimmy!' said Mike. 'We tried to get you out of prison sooner. But the Springfield police made trouble for us. Here's the key to your room.'

Mike gave him a key and Jimmy went upstairs to his room. He unlocked the door and he went inside. Nothing in the room had changed. Nobody had been inside it for nine months.

The police had arrested Jimmy in this room. Jimmy had fought them and one of Ben Price's shirt-buttons had come off in the fight. The great detective's button was still on the floor of the room.

Jimmy Valentine smiled. Then he pulled a dusty suitcase from behind the bed. He opened it carefully. Inside the case was the best set of burglar's tools in the United States. Jimmy had paid $900 for them! He had made some of the tools himself.

Half an hour later, Jimmy went downstairs again. He was wearing smart clothes and his suitcase was clean and bright.

'Are you going to do another job?' asked Mike.

'Me?' said Jimmy. 'A job? I don't understand you, Mike. I sell biscuits. I'm a salesman for the New York Cracker Company!'

Jimmy laughed. Mike laughed too.

———

One week later, there was a burglary in Richmond, Indiana. The burglar took $800 from an old safe. Two weeks after that, somebody stole $1500 from a new safe in Logansport, Indiana. Then $5000 disappeared from a safe in a bank in Jefferson City, Missouri.

Ben Price investigated these three burglaries.

'Jimmy Valentine is working again!' he said.

Ben Price knew all about Jimmy Valentine. Jimmy worked alone. And he travelled many miles between jobs. Jimmy moved fast. And he enjoyed good clothes, good food and fine wine.

'I'll catch him,' the detective said to himself. 'And next time, he'll stay in prison. Next time, there will be no government pardon for him.'

———

One afternoon, Jimmy and his suitcase arrived at the little town of Elmore. Elmore was in Arkansas. The town was five miles from the nearest railroad station.

Jimmy walked along Elmore's main street. He was young. He was handsome. He wore good clothes. Not many young men in Elmore were as good-looking as Jimmy Valentine.

A beautiful young lady walked along the street

towards him. Jimmy Valentine looked into her eyes –
and he fell in love. The young lady's cheeks became
red. She passed him. Jimmy turned and watched her
entering the Elmore Bank.

A boy was playing in the street outside the bank.
Jimmy gave the boy a coin and asked him some ques-
tions about the town. After a few minutes, the young
lady came out of the bank.

Jimmy gave the boy another coin. 'Who is that
young lady?' he asked.

'She's Miss Annabel Adams,' replied the boy. 'Her father owns the bank.'

Jimmy walked to the Planters' Hotel and he asked for a room.

'My name is Ralph D. Spencer,' he told the hotel clerk. 'I want to start a business here. Is there a shoe store in Elmore?'

'No, there isn't a shoe store here,' the clerk replied. 'This town needs a shoe store. You'll like Elmore, Mr Spencer. The people here are very friendly.'

'I'll stay for a few days,' said Jimmy. 'I'll look around the town.'

'Do you want someone to carry your suitcase up the stairs?' asked the clerk.

'No, I'll carry it myself,' Jimmy replied. 'It's very heavy.'

———

'Mr Ralph Spencer' stayed in Elmore. Soon, he owned a small shoe store in the town. The store was success-ful. People liked Mr Spencer and they respected him. He made many friends. And soon, he met Miss Annabel Adams.

At the end of the year, Ralph D. Spencer and Annabel Adams were engaged to be married.

Annabel loved Ralph Spencer and she was proud of him. And her father, the owner of the Elmore Bank, liked Ralph very much too. The Adams family often invited him to their home.

———

One day, two weeks before the wedding day, Jimmy was sitting in his room at the Planters' Hotel. He thought for a while, then he wrote a letter. It was a letter to a friend in St Louis, Missouri.

Planters' Hotel, Elmore

Tuesday

Dear Billy,

Please meet me at Sullivan's Bar in Little Rock, Arkansas, next Wednesday night. I want to give you my tools. I'm an honest man now. I've got a nice shoe store in this town. And, in two weeks, I'm going to marry the best girl in the world. She believes in me. She trusts me and she is proud of me.

I'll never do another wrong thing. Please come to Sullivan's Bar. I'll bring the tools with me.

Your friend,

Jimmy Valentine

The next Monday, Ben Price arrived in Elmore. The detective talked to many people.

He asked them about Jimmy Valentine. Nobody in the town knew Jimmy Valentine. But everybody talked about Ralph D. Spencer.

Soon, Ben Price started to watch the owner of the shoe store.

'Jimmy! You're going to marry the banker's daughter,' the detective said to himself. 'That's very interesting!'

On Tuesday morning, Jimmy had breakfast at the banker's house, outside the town.

'I'm going to Little Rock today,' he told the family. 'I want to buy my wedding-suit. And I want to buy something nice for Annabel.'

'I want you to see something at the bank first,' said Mr Adams.

After breakfast, they all walked into the town together – Mr Adams, Jimmy, Annabel and Annabel's sister with her two little girls. They stopped at the Planters' Hotel and Jimmy brought his suitcase from his room. Then they all walked on towards the bank.

Inside the bank, Jimmy put down his suitcase. Annabel tried to lift it. She laughed.

'Ralph, your case is very heavy!' she said.

'Yes, my dear,' Jimmy replied. 'There are lots of heavy shoes in it.'

Mr Adams took his family and Jimmy behind the high railings, into the banking-room.

Elmore Bank had a new strong-room. Mr Adams was very proud of it. He wanted to show the new strong-room to his family, and to his friend, Ralph Spencer.

'Some men from a company in Little Rock built it,' Mr Adams said. 'They finished it yesterday.'

The strong-room had a very thick steel door. There was a special lock on the door – a combination lock. The banker explained about the lock to his friend.

'This is a combination lock,' he said. 'There isn't a key. The numbers on those four knobs unlock the door. But we mustn't close the door. I haven't chosen the numbers for the combination.'

Everybody was interested in the strong-room. The two little girls, May and Agatha, loved the shiny metal door. They loved the big, shiny handle. And they loved the knobs with numbers on them.

———

Ben Price had seen the banker's family enter the bank with Jimmy. After a few minutes, the great detective followed them into the building.

Ben Price looked through the railings, into the banking-room.

'Good morning, sir,' one of the clerks said to him. 'Do you need some help?'

'No, thank you,' said the detective. 'I'm waiting for someone. I'm going to meet a friend here.'

Behind the railings, Annabel and her sister suddenly screamed. May, the sister's older child, had closed the door of the strong-room. Then she had turned all the knobs. But the other child, Agatha, was inside the strong-room!

Mr Adams ran to the steel door. He pulled the big handle.

'I can't open it!' he shouted. 'Nobody has chosen the numbers for the lock!'

'Oh, what shall we do?' Annabel's sister asked.

'There isn't much air in the strong-room,' Mr Adams said. 'I must send for a man from the lock company. But the company is in Little Rock!'

Agatha's mother screamed again. 'My darling will die!'

Mr Adams' face was white. 'Please be quiet, everybody,' he said. Then he shouted through the thick steel door.

'Agatha!' he shouted. 'Agatha! Listen to me. We'll get you out of there soon!'

The child was alone in the dark strong-room. She was only five years old and she was very frightened. The family heard her crying.

19

Jimmy put the rose in his coat pocket. Then he took off his coat and he pulled up the sleeves of his shirt. And suddenly, Ralph D. Spencer, the owner of the shoe store, became Jimmy Valentine, the safe-cracker!

'Everybody must move away from the strong-room door,' he said.

Jimmy lifted his suitcase onto a table and opened it. Quickly and carefully, he took out the strange, shiny tools. He sang quietly to himself. Everybody watched him. Nobody spoke.

After a few minutes, one of Jimmy's special tools was cutting into the steel door. After ten minutes, he had cut out the locks. And one minute after that, Jimmy pulled the big handle and the door opened.

Little Agatha fell into her mother's arms. The child was frightened but she was not hurt.

Jimmy Valentine had cracked the strong-room door in less than fifteen minutes. It was the fastest job of his life.

Jimmy put on his coat. He walked through the banking-room, towards the street door. He heard a young woman's voice behind him.

'Ralph! Come back!'

But Jimmy did not turn round.

A big man was standing in front of the door. It was Ben Price.

'Hello, Ben!' said Jimmy. 'You've found me. I won't fight you this time. Arrest me. Take me away. I don't care any more.'

Ben Price looked past Jimmy. He looked at Annabel. He looked at the mother and her children in the banking-room. They were all crying quietly.

'You've made a mistake, Mr – Mr Spencer,' the detective said. 'I don't understand you.'

Then the great detective turned and walked out of the bank.

2
THE LAST LEAF

In the 1890s, many artists lived in Greenwich Village, in New York City.

Sue and Johnsy were artists. The two girls first met each other in the month of May, at a restaurant in Greenwich Village.

'I'm from the state of Maine,' Sue said to Johnsy. 'I draw pictures for stories in magazines.'

'I'm from California,' Johnsy said to Sue. 'But I want to go to Italy. I want to paint a picture of the Bay of Naples!'

The two girls talked happily for an hour – about art, about clothes, about food.

Soon after their first meeting, Sue and Johnsy moved into a studio apartment together. Their rooms were at the top of an old brick house in Greenwich village.

In December, it was very cold in New York. Snow fell and there was ice on the ground. Many people in the city became ill. The illness was called pneumonia. The doctors tried to help the sick people, but many of them died.

That month, Johnsy had pneumonia. She was very ill. She lay in her bed and she did not move. A doctor visited her every day. But Johnsy was not getting better.

One morning, the doctor spoke quietly to Sue outside Johnsy's room.

'I can't help her,' the doctor said. 'She is very sad. She doesn't want to live. Someone must make her happy again. What is she interested in?'

'She's an artist,' Sue replied. 'She wants to paint a picture of the Bay of Naples.'

'Painting!' said the doctor. 'That won't help her!'

The doctor left the apartment.

Sue went into her own room and she cried quietly for a few minutes. Then she picked up her drawing-board and some pencils. She started to sing a happy song and she walked into Johnsy's room.

Johnsy lay silently in her bed. Her face was thin and white. She was looking towards the window.

'Johnsy is asleep,' Sue thought.

She stopped singing and she sat down in a corner of the room. Then she started to draw a picture for a magazine. Suddenly, Sue heard a quiet sound. She went quickly to the side of the bed. Johnsy's eyes were open. She was looking out of the window and she was speaking quietly.

'Twelve,' Johnsy said. A little later, she said 'eleven'. Then she said 'ten'. Then 'nine'. And then she said 'eight' and 'seven' almost together. She was counting backwards.

What was Johnsy looking at? What was she counting? Sue looked out of the window.

Outside the window, Sue saw the brick wall of the next house. An old vine grew against the wall. There were very few leaves on its branches.

'Six,' Johnsy said. 'They're falling faster. Three days ago, there were almost a hundred. Ah, there goes another! There are only five now.'

'Five? What are you talking about, Johnsy?' Sue asked. 'Please tell me.'

'There are only five leaves on the vine now,' said Johnsy. 'The last leaf will fall soon and then I'll die. Didn't the doctor tell you about the leaves?'

'Don't say that! You're not going to die!' Sue said. 'You're going to get better. The doctor told me that this morning. I'll bring you some soup and I'll draw my picture. The magazine will pay me quickly. Then I'll buy us some nice food.'

Johnsy was still looking at the vine. 'There are only four leaves now,' she said. 'I don't want any soup. The last leaf will fall soon.'

'Johnsy, dear,' Sue said. 'Please close your eyes and go to sleep. I have to finish this drawing by tomorrow. And I don't want you to look at those leaves any more.'

Johnsy closed her eyes. 'But I want to watch the last leaf,' she said again. 'It will fall soon. The leaves are tired. I'm tired too. I want to die.'

'Please try to sleep,' Sue said. 'I'm going to talk to Behrman for a minute. I must have a model for my drawing. Behrman will be my model.'

Old Behrman lived downstairs. He was also an artist, but he had never painted a good picture. He was sad about this and he was angry about it too.

'One day, I will paint a wonderful picture,' Behrman often said. 'One day, I will paint a masterpiece.'

But he had never painted a masterpiece. And he was more than sixty years old.

Sue found the little old man in his dark room. She told him about Johnsy and the vine leaves.

'Oh, the foolish girl!' Behrman shouted. 'An old vine can't kill people!'

'But the vine *is* killing her,' said Sue. 'She's very ill and weak. She sees the vine dying. Now she wants to die too.'

Behrman was angry, but he loved the two young artists very much.

'Ah, little Miss Johnsy,' he said quietly. 'She's too good for this place. One day, I will paint a masterpiece. Then we will all go to Italy. We will go to Naples. Yes! But today, I'll be your model.'

Together, they went upstairs. Johnsy was sleeping. Sue pulled the shade down over her friend's bedroom window. Then she took Behrman into her own room. They both looked out of the window. They looked at the vine. Cold rain was falling.

'Soon there will be snow,' Sue thought. Behrman sat down and Sue started to draw a picture of him.

———

That night, there was a storm. The rain fell heavily and the wind was very strong.

Johnsy woke early the next morning. 'Pull up the shade,' she said to Sue.

Sue pulled up the shade. There was still one leaf on the vine! The leaf was dark green and yellow. And it hung from a branch twenty feet above the ground.

'That's the last leaf,' said Johnsy. 'It will fall today. I'll die at the same time.'

Sue put her face close to her friend's face.

'Don't say that, Johnsy,' she said quietly. 'I don't want you to die.'

Johnsy did not answer.

The leaf stayed on the vine all day. That night, there was more wind and rain.

In the morning, Johnsy woke early again. 'Pull up the shade,' she said.

The leaf was still on the vine. Johnsy lay in her bed and she looked at it for a long time. Then she called to Sue.

'I've been a very foolish girl, Sue,' she said. 'I wanted to die. But the last leaf has stayed on the vine. It has taught me a lesson. Please, bring me a bowl of soup now.'

An hour later, Johnsy spoke again.

'Sue, my dear,' she said. 'One day, I'm going to paint a picture of the Bay of Naples!'

———

The doctor visited the girls in the afternoon. He looked at Johnsy carefully and he held Sue's thin hand.

'Take good care of your friend,' he said. 'She is going to get well. Now I have to go downstairs. I have to visit Mr Behrman. He has pneumonia too. I must send him to the hospital.'

———

The next day, the doctor spoke to Sue again.

'Your friend will soon be well,' he said. Then he told her some other news.

That afternoon, Sue went into Johnsy's room and she put her arm around her friend's shoulders.

'Mr Behrman died this morning, in the hospital,' she said. 'Two days ago, one of the neighbours found him in his bedroom. Behrman was very ill. His shoes and clothes were cold and wet. The neighbour sent for the doctor. Later, the neighbour found a ladder outside in the yard. There was a lamp next to it. And there were brushes, and some yellow and green paint.'

'Johnsy, look out of the window,' Sue said quietly. 'Look at the last leaf on the vine. It's still there. It has never moved in the wind. Didn't that surprise you? It's Behrman's masterpiece, dear. He painted it on the night of the storm.'

3

A LESSON IN LOVE

Joe and Delia were students. They both loved Art. They both lived for Art!

Joe had always loved painting pictures. At the age of twenty, he had left his family's home in Kansas and he had come to New York City. He had very little money, but he was very ambitious.

'One day, I'll be a famous artist,' he always said.

Delia had always loved playing the piano. She had left her family's home in Missouri and she too had come to New York. Her family had given her some money. She was very ambitious too.

'One day, I'll be a famous pianist,' she always said. 'I'll play the piano at concerts.'

In New York, Joe and Delia met other art students and music students. And very soon, Joe and Delia met each other. They fell in love and they got married.

After their marriage, Joe and Delia lived in a studio apartment. It was a small, cheap apartment in Lower Manhattan. They both worked hard every day. Joe was having painting lessons from the famous painter, Mr Magister. Delia was having piano lessons from the famous pianist, Mr Rosenstock.

Joe and Delia were poor, but they were happy. Some people will do anything for Art! Joe and Delia had their Art and they had each other. Life was wonderful!

Every morning, Joe and Delia had their breakfast together. Then they went happily to their lessons. Every evening, they had supper in their apartment and they talked about their plans.

'Soon, people will buy my pictures,' said Joe.

'Soon, people will come to my concerts,' said Delia.

But after a few months, Art was not enough. Joe and Delia were very poor. Lessons from Mr Magister and Mr Rosenstock were very expensive.

'I'm not going to have any more piano lessons, Joe dear,' Delia told her husband one evening. 'I am going to teach music. Artists have to eat!'

Three evenings later, Delia came home with a smile on her face.

'Joe dear, I'm going to teach a music student!' she said. 'Her name is Clementina. She's eighteen years old and she lives on Seventy-first Street. Her father is General A.B. Pinkney.'

'Clementina is very sweet,' Delia said. 'But she's not very strong. The General wants me to give her three lessons a week. And he's going to pay me five dollars a lesson! Yes! Soon I will go back to Mr Rosenstock.'

Delia looked at her husband's face. Joe was not happy about her news.

'Please, don't be angry, Joe,' she said. 'Let's have a nice supper.'

Joe opened a can of peas.

'You're going to teach a student,' he said sadly. 'And I will stop going to Mr Magister, Delia. I will sell newspapers and I'll earn a few dollars.'

Delia put her arms around her husband's neck.

'Joe dear, don't be foolish,' she said. 'You mustn't leave Mr Magister. We can live very well on fifteen dollars a week.'

Joe put the peas into a dish.

'All right. You're a dear girl,' he said to his wife. 'But I don't like it. Teaching isn't Art!'

'I will teach for the *love* of Art!' Delia replied. 'We'll do anything for the love of Art!'

After a moment, Joe spoke.

'Mr Magister liked the sky in my painting of Central

Park,' he said. 'And he showed two of my pictures to an art dealer, Mr Tinkle. Mr Tinkle is going to put my pictures in his shop window. Soon, somebody will buy one of them.'

'Yes, somebody will buy one,' said Delia sweetly. 'Thank you, General Pinkney, and thank you too, Mr Tinkle. We *will* live for Art. And now, let's eat these nice peas and drink a cup of tea.'

The next week, Joe painted in Central Park every day. Every day, he and Delia ate their breakfast early. Then Delia kissed him and said goodbye to him. At seven o'clock in the morning, he left the apartment. He did not come back until seven o'clock in the evening. Some people will do anything for the love of Art!

On Saturday evening, Joe arrived home first. Delia arrived soon after him. She put fifteen dollars on the dining-table in the small apartment. She was tired but she was proud.

'Clementina doesn't work hard enough,' she said to Joe. 'I have to tell her the same things at every lesson. But she's very sweet. And General Pinkney is a dear old man! He comes into the music-room sometimes and he listens to us.'

Then Joe took eighteen dollars from his pocket. He put the money next to Delia's money on the table.

'I sold a painting to a man from Peoria,' he said.

'You sold a painting?' said Delia. 'To a man from Peoria, Illinois? That's wonderful, Joe!'

'That's right, Delia,' Joe replied. 'A fat man from Peoria, Illinois, bought a painting. He saw it in Mr Tinkle's window and he bought it. Now he wants another of my paintings too. Soon, you won't have to teach music any more. We will live for Art again!'

'Oh, Joe,' said Delia. 'One day, you'll be famous. And tonight we've got thirty-three dollars! What shall we eat for supper? I'll go to the stores.'

'We'll have the best beef,' said Joe. 'And a bottle of wine.'

The next Saturday evening, Joe arrived home first again. He was very tired. His hands were dirty and black. He washed them quickly. Then he put eighteen dollars on the table.

A moment later, Delia arrived at the apartment. There was a bandage on her right hand.

'What's happened to you, Delia?' asked Joe. 'Have you hurt your hand?'

Delia tried to laugh.

'Clementina wasn't well today,' she said. 'She spilt

some hot tea on my hand. The dear girl was very sorry! And General Pinkney sent a servant to a drugstore for some bandages. My hand hurt terribly at first, Joe. But it doesn't hurt much now.'

Joe held her hand gently.

'What's this?' he asked. He was looking at a piece of white cloth under the bandage.

'It's a piece of soft cloth with oil on it,' said Delia.

Then she saw the eighteen dollars on the table.

'Oh, Joe, did you sell another picture?' she asked.

'Yes! The fat man from Peoria bought his second painting today!' Joe said. 'And he wants two more. But when did you burn your hand, Delia?'

'At five o'clock this afternoon,' Delia replied. 'The iron – no, the tea —'

'Sit down, Delia,' said Joe. He put his arm around his wife's shoulders. 'What have you been doing for the last two weeks?' he asked.

For a moment or two, Delia talked about General Pinkney and Clementina. But then she started to cry.

'Oh, Joe,' she said. 'There is no General Pinkney. There is no Clementina. I couldn't get any students. But I didn't want you to stop your lessons with Mr Magister. I got a job in that big laundry on Twenty-fourth Street. I iron shirts there. But this afternoon, one of the girls dropped a hot iron on my hand.'

She looked up at her husband. 'Don't be angry with me,' she said. 'Kiss me, Joe. How clever you are! How did you guess about General Pinkney?'

'I didn't guess until tonight,' said Joe. 'Then I saw the piece of cloth on your hand, under the bandage. I saw the cloth with oil on it. I sent that piece of cloth up from the boiler-room this afternoon. I sent it for one of the girls upstairs. I've worked in the boiler-room of that laundry for two weeks. I put coal into the boilers.'

'You didn't sell any pictures?' asked Delia.

'No,' Joe replied sadly. 'There is no fat man from Peoria!'

Suddenly, they both laughed.

'Oh, Delia,' Joe said. 'Two weeks ago, you told me, "We'll do anything for the love of Art." Do you remember?'

Delia put her hand on her husband's lips.

'Yes, but I was wrong, Joe,' she said. 'We'll do anything for Love.'

40

4

THE JEWELLER'S WIFE

Mr Thomas Keeling wanted to be a private detective. Many people needed private detectives. Sometimes, a businessman wanted somebody to investigate his clerk. Was the clerk stealing his money? Sometimes, a lady wanted somebody to watch her husband. Was her husband meeting another woman? The businessman and the wife both needed a private detective. People needed Mr Thomas Keeling!

Mr Keeling was a quiet, serious man. He wanted to do his job well. He had read many books about famous detectives. He had saved $900. He was going to start a business.

One day, Mr Keeling came to Houston, Texas. He rented a small office in a quiet street. He put a sign outside his office and he waited for his first client.

For three days, Mr Keeling sat in his office and he read detective stories. But on the fourth day, a client came up the stairs to the office.

Mr Keeling looked at his client carefully. He saw a young lady. She was about twenty-five years old. She was tall and slim. Her black clothes were smart. She wore a black hat. A thin black veil covered her face.

'Good afternoon, madam,' said Mr Keeling. 'Please sit down.'

The lady lifted her veil.

Her face was lovely and she had large, grey eyes.

The lady spoke in a sad, soft voice.

'You are a stranger in this city, sir,' she said. 'That is the reason for my visit. I have a problem. I cannot speak about it to any of my friends. Mr Keeling, I want you to watch my husband.'

'Please tell me about your problem,' said Mr Keeling.

'My name is Mrs Robbins,' the lady said. 'My husband is a well-known man in this city. He has a small jewellery store on Main Street. We have been married for five years. But my husband does not love me any more. He meets another woman secretly.'

Mr Keeling listened carefully. He said nothing.

'I want you to watch my husband,' Mrs Robbins said again. 'I want you to tell me about his movements. I will come to your office every second day. You will give me your reports. I will pay you well.'

She held out twenty dollars.

Mr Keeling took the money.

'I will help you, Mrs Robbins,' he said. 'Come here the day after tomorrow, at four o'clock. I'll give you my first report then. Good afternoon, dear lady.'

———

The detective began his investigation the next morning. He went to the jewellery store on Main Street. He entered the store and he looked around. The owner of the store was working behind the counter.

The jeweller, Mr Robbins, was about thirty-five years old. His store was small, but there were beautiful diamonds, expensive necklaces and fine watches on the shelves.

Good morning, sir.

Good morning. I need a new chain for my watch.

Later, the detective stood in the street near the jewellery store for several hours. At last, something happened.

A young woman came along the street and she entered the store. She had black hair and dark eyes. Her clothes were bright and colourful.

Mr Keeling went nearer to the store and he looked through the window. The young woman walked up to the counter. She said something to Mr Robbins. He stopped working and the two of them talked quietly for a few minutes. Then the jeweller gave the woman some coins. A moment later, she came out of the store and she walked quickly down the street.

———

At four o'clock the next afternoon, Mr Keeling's client came to his office.

'What did you find out about my husband?' she asked.

'I saw a woman go into the jewellery store,' said Mr Keeling. 'Your husband gave her some money. She was a young, dark-eyed woman. Her hair was black and her clothes were colourful.'

'That's her!' said the lady. 'Charles is giving her money! That's terrible!'

The lady held a handkerchief over her eyes. She was crying.

'Mrs Robbins, what do you want me to do now?' asked the detective. 'Do you want me to continue this investigation?'

'I want to see my husband and this terrible woman together,' replied the lady. 'I also want witnesses – I want other people to see them together. Then I want to end our marriage – I want a divorce.'

She gave the detective ten dollars.

'I shall come for your second report the day after tomorrow,' she said. 'I'll come at four o'clock.'

———

Two days later, the lady came to the detective's office for the second report.

'Please sit down, Mrs Robbins. I have some news for you,' said Mr Keeling. 'I went into the jewellery store again this afternoon. The young woman was already there. I heard her speaking to your husband.'

'My husband is a terrible man!' the detective's client said angrily. 'He lies to me about his work!'

'Mrs Robbins,' said Mr Keeling. 'Tonight, you must watch the meeting between your husband and this young woman. You must hide in the store and you must listen to their words.'

'Yes! I'll do it!' said the lady. 'A policeman lives in this street. He is a kind man. He knows my family. Please find him. Tell him about my husband. He must come with you to the store tonight. You and he will be my witnesses.'

'I'll speak to him,' said the detective. 'Please come here again at seven o'clock. Then we'll go to the store together.'

Mrs Robbins left the office. Mr Keeling found the policeman's house and he knocked on the door.

The detective explained his plan. He asked the policeman for his help.

'Mrs Robbins wants to catch her husband with this woman,' he said. 'Tonight, Mrs Robbins is going to hide in the store. She is going to listen to their words. And she wants you to be a witness. But we have a problem. First, she has to get into the store.'

'I'll help the lady,' said the policeman. 'Let me think about your problem. Yes! I have the answer! There's a little room at the back of the store. She must enter by that door. But the door between that room and the store is always locked. You'll have to open it for her.'

———

At seven o'clock that evening, the detective's client came to his office for the fourth time. Again, she was wearing black clothes and there was a veil over her face. After a few minutes, they went out into the street together.

Mr Keeling and the lady walked slowly along the sidewalk. They stopped opposite the jewellery store. They waited. At about eight o'clock, a young woman entered the store. After a few minutes, she came out again with Mr Robbins. She was holding his arm. They walked away, down the street.

The lady in black began to cry quietly.

'Look at them!' she said. 'My terrible husband and that bad young woman!'

Mr Keeling took his client to the back yard of the

store. The lady opened a door in the wall and they entered the small room behind the store.

The detective and his client crossed the room to a locked door.

'This is the door into the store,' said the lady.

'Where are you going to hide?' the detective asked.

'I want to hide in the store,' the lady replied. 'In the store, there is a large table. A cloth covers the table, and it hangs down to the floor. I'll hide under the table. I'll listen to my husband and that woman. I'll hear every word. But how can I get into the store? This door is locked.'

Mr Keeling took some special keys from his pocket. He tried to open the door with them. He put one key after another into the lock. At last, one of the keys unlocked the door. The lady went into the store. Mr Keeling did not follow her.

'I'll lock the door from this side,' the lady told the detective. 'Give me your key. You must go now. Find my husband and that woman. Then get the policeman and follow them back to the store. I'll listen to my husband and that woman from under the table. Then I'll come out from under the table. I'll open the street door. You and the policeman will come into the store. You will both be my witnesses.'

Mr Keeling soon found the jeweller and the young woman. They were eating in a quiet restaurant. He waited in the street. After a few minutes, Mr Robbins and the young woman left the restaurant.

The detective went quickly to the policeman's house. Then the two men hurried to the jewellery store. They looked through the window. The policeman was surprised. He spoke to Mr Keeling.

'I don't understand,' said the policeman. 'You told me, "Robbins took a young woman to a restaurant." Where is she?'

'*There she is!*' said Mr Keeling. He pointed through the window.

'Do you know the lady with Robbins?' asked the policeman.

'That's his secret friend,' said Mr Keeling.

'No! You're wrong! That's Robbins' wife,' said the policeman. 'I've known her for fifteen years.'

'*What?*' the detective shouted. His face became pale. 'Who is under the table in the store?'

He started to kick the door of the jewellery store.

Mr Robbins came to the door and opened it. The policeman and the detective ran into the store.

'Look under that table!' shouted the detective. 'Look under the cloth. Be quick!'

The policeman lifted the cloth and put his arm under the table. He pulled out a black dress, a black veil and a woman's wig.

'Is this young lady your wife?' Mr Keeling asked the jeweller. He pointed at the woman.

'Yes! She is my wife!' said Mr Robbins angrily. 'Why did you kick my door? Why are those clothes under my table?'

'Please check all the jewellery in your store, Mr Robbins,' the policeman said. 'Is anything missing?'

Some diamond rings and some expensive necklaces were missing. Some watches were missing too. The missing jewellery was worth $800.

Later that night, Mr Keeling was sitting in his office. He was looking through a big book of photographs. They were photographs of criminals. The policeman had brought the book to the detective's office. Suddenly, Mr Keeling stopped turning the pages. He looked at a picture of a good-looking young man with a smooth face. He read the words underneath the photograph.

JAMES H. MIGGLES, also known as 'The Unhappy Wife'.

Description: Tall and slim. Grey eyes.

Crime: Burglary.

Miggles usually wears women's clothes. He is clever and dangerous. The police in Kansas City, New Orleans and Chicago are searching for him.

The next morning, Mr Keeling paid the jeweller $800, then he closed his office.

Mr Thomas Keeling, private detective, does not work in Houston any more.

5

THE CAR IS WAITING

It was a warm, quiet evening. A young woman came into a little park in New York City. Her fine grey dress was plain and she wore a small grey hat with a veil. Behind the veil, her face was calm and beautiful. She sat down on a seat and she started to read a book.

Every day that week, the young woman had come to the same place at the same time. And every day, a young man had seen her there. This evening, he was waiting near the seat. He watched the young woman sit down. He watched her reading her book.

Suddenly, the young woman dropped the book. The young man ran towards her. He picked up the book and he gave it to her.

'It's a lovely evening,' he said.

For a moment, the woman in grey looked at the young man calmly. Then she spoke to him. Her voice was beautiful too.

'Sit down on this seat,' she said carefully. 'I cannot read now. We will talk together for a few minutes.'

The young man quickly sat down next to her. His clothes and his face were ordinary. His next words were ordinary too.

'You're a lovely girl,' he said. 'You're a beauty! I saw you here yesterday. Did you see me, little flower?'

The young woman looked at the man coldly.

'I do not know you,' she said. 'But I am a lady. Please remember that. Please do not call me "little flower" again.'

'I'm very sorry,' said the young man. 'But other girls in parks —'

'I know nothing about other young women in parks,' she said. 'I know nothing about the ordinary world, Mr —?'

'My name is Parkenstacker,' said the young man. 'And your name is —?'

The young woman shook her head.

'I shall not tell you my name,' she said. 'My name and my face are well known. My picture is often in newspapers and magazines. But I come here secretly. This dress and hat and veil belong to my maid. I am not an ordinary person. I know nothing about the ordinary world, Mr Stackenparker —'

'Parkenstacker,' said the young man.

'Mr Parkenstacker. I know nothing about the ordinary world,' the young woman said again. 'But I want to meet some ordinary people. I come here every day for that reason. I spoke to you today for that reason. I wanted to talk to somebody without money and without power. Oh, I am tired of money! I am tired of rich men! I am tired of jewels!'

The young man was very surprised.

'But isn't money nice?' he asked.

'A little money is good,' the young woman answered. 'But millions and millions of dollars are very boring! Travelling, dinners, plays, dances – again and again and again! Sometimes, the sound of the ice in my champagne glass tires me!'

Mr Parkenstacker was surprised again.

'Do rich people put ice in their champagne?' he asked. 'Don't they put ice around the bottle?'

For a moment, the young woman was angry. Then she laughed.

'It's a new fashion,' she said. 'This week, we all put ice in our champagne. The Prince of Tartary did it last week, at the Waldorf Hotel. And now we all do it!'

'I'm sorry,' said the young man. 'I know nothing about princes.'

'And I know too much about them,' said the young woman. 'Princes, dukes – they all fall in love with me. Last week, a German duke wanted to marry me. He met me at the Waldorf Hotel. He said, "I want you to be my wife." But I do not love him. I do not love anybody, Mr Packenstarker.'

'Parkenstacker!' said the young man. He looked into the young woman's eyes. 'Can you love an ordinary man?' he asked her.

The young woman looked at him calmly. 'What work do you do?' she asked.

'I do a very ordinary job,' the young man replied. 'But can you love an ordinary man?'

'It is possible,' she said. 'But I asked you a question. What work do you do? Please answer me.'

'I work in a restaurant,' said Mr Parkenstacker.

The woman in grey moved along the seat, away from the young man.

'Are you a waiter?' she asked.

'No. I'm not a waiter,' he replied. 'Do you see that restaurant?'

The young man pointed to a large restaurant in the street, opposite the little park. It had bright electric signs in its windows.

'I work there,' he said. 'I'm a cashier. The customers in that restaurant pay their money to me.'

Suddenly, the young woman was worried. She looked at a little watch on her wrist and she got up quickly. She put her book into a small bag.

'I must go now,' she said. 'I must go to a boring dinner and then I must go to the theatre. My car is at the corner of the park.'

'That big white car?' asked the young man. 'Is that your car?'

'Yes, I always come here in the white car,' the young woman replied. 'Pierre, my driver, waits for me. Goodnight.'

'Shall I see you again?' asked Mr Parkenstacker.

'I do not know,' the woman in grey replied.

'It's late now, and it's dark,' the young man said. 'I will walk with you to —'

'No!' said the young woman. 'Please stay on this seat for ten minutes. My family's name is on the doors of the car. I do not want you to know our name. Please stay here. Goodnight, Mr Parkenstacker.'

The woman in grey walked quickly towards the street.

The young man watched her for half a minute.

Then he followed her out of the little park.

The young woman walked up to the white car. She stopped and she looked at it for a few moments. Then she passed it and she ran across the street. She entered the restaurant with the bright electric signs.

The young woman went through a door at the back of the restaurant. After a minute, she came back into the room without her hat and veil.

The cashier's desk was at the front of the restaurant. A young woman with red hair was sitting at the desk. Suddenly, she looked at her watch. Then she saw the woman in grey and she got off the chair. The woman in grey sat at the desk.

In the street opposite the restaurant, the young man walked slowly along the sidewalk. He saw a book lying on the ground. It was the young woman's book. It had fallen out of her bag. He picked it up and he looked at it. It was a book of romances. The stories in the book were about poor young women. In the stories, these women married princes and dukes and rich men with fine houses.

The young man dropped the book. He stood on the sidewalk for a moment. Then he walked to the big white car and he got into it.

'Take me home, Henri,' he said to the driver.

Published by Macmillan Heinemann ELT
Between Towns Road, Oxford, OX4 3PP
Macmillan Heinemann ELT is an imprint of
Macmillan Publishers Limited

Companies and representatives throughout the world

ISBN 0 333 75727 0

This retold version by Katherine Mattock for Macmillan Guided Readers
Text © Katherine Mattock 1999, 2002
Design and illustration © Macmillan Publishers Limited 1999, 2002
First published 1999
Heinemann is a registered trademark of Reed Educational & Professional Publishing Limited
This version first published 2002

'A Good Burglar' was originally entitled 'A Retrieved Reformation',
'A Lesson in Love' was originally entitled 'A Service of Love', 'The Jeweller's Wife'
was originally entitled 'The Dissipated Jeweller' and 'The Car is Waiting' was
originally entitled 'While the Auto Waits'. These stories were first published
together in *The Complete Works of O. Henry* in 1928.

Acknowledgements: The publishers would like to thank Hulton Getty for
permission to reproduce the picture on page 4.

Illustrated by Philip Bannister
Map on page 7 by Peter Harper
Cover by Mandy Pritty and Marketplace Design

Printed in China

2003 2002
10 9 8 7 6 5 4